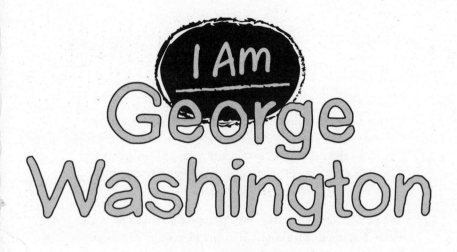

I Am George Washington

By Grace Norwich

Illustrated by
Anthony VanArsdale

SCHOLASTIC INC.

ISBN 978-0-545-48435-0

10 9 8 7 6   15 16 17/0

Printed in the U.S.A.   40
First printing, December 2012

Cover illustration by Mark Fredrickson
Interior illustrations by Anthony VanArsdale

Contents

Introduction

When I was a boy, I spent a long time carefully copying a list of rules into my notebook. These were what I called rules of civility, and they were important far after I first committed them to memory.

I lived by these sound rules my whole life. But one rule—Rule 82—particularly comes to mind when I think back about both my adventures leading the ragtag American army against the British superpower in the Revolutionary War, and also becoming the first president of the United States of America. "Undertake not what you cannot perform," the rule states, "but be careful to keep your promise." Basically, don't go around saying you can do a lot of stuff you can't.

See, my whole life, I didn't seek out being in charge. I *did* want to find adventure (and boy, did I find that!). But whenever people nominated me to lead troops into battle or later take on the highest office in the country, I questioned their judgment. They said I was a leader, brave, honest, fearless, and just. My thoughts of myself were much more modest.

Every time I was asked to serve my country, whether becoming commander in chief of the Continental army or serving two terms as president, I had serious doubts about my abilities to take on those tasks with the highest skill they required.

My deep sense of patriotism and duty always drove me to push myself further than I thought was possible. And in the end, it served me well as I led the new country I loved so much.

I'm remembered as a war hero, statesman, and patriot. Still, I think my **humility** is one of my most important and often overlooked qualities. It's what allowed me to keep my head on straight when some Americans wanted to make me a king instead of a president. I refused because I knew that the strength of the United States and the value of **liberty** were more powerful than any one person—even me. I am George Washington.

People You Will Meet

GEORGE WASHINGTON:
A Virginian, who led troops into battle during the French and Indian War, became commander in chief during the Revolutionary War, and then became the first president of the United States.

AUGUSTINE WASHINGTON:
George's father, better known as Gus, came from a long line of tobacco growers in Virginia and died when George was only eleven.

MARY WASHINGTON:
George's mother, also a native Virginian, was a cold, difficult woman who never grew close to or acted proud of her son.

LAWRENCE WASHINGTON: George's half brother who took him under his wing and into his home, Mount Vernon.

MARTHA WASHINGTON: The wealthy widow became George's wife after he returned from the French and Indian War, and remained his loving companion until his death.

THOMAS JEFFERSON: Also from Virginia, the Founding Father drafted the Declaration of Independence, encouraged George to run for president, and later became the third president.

KING GEORGE III: The grandson of King George II, this ruler of Britain decided to tax the colonies to pay for the expensive French and Indian War, setting off the Revolution.

JACKY: Martha's son from a previous marriage, whom George treated as his own.

PATSY: Martha's daughter from a previous marriage. She died at age seventeen.

Time Line

February 22, 1732

George is born to Augustine and Mary Washington.

April 12, 1743

George's father dies.

May 28, 1754

The French and Indian War begins. During the war, George leads an attack on France's largest fort.

January 6, 1759

George and Martha Custis, a widowed mother of two, are married.

December 16, 1773

The Sons of Liberty throw English tea into Boston Harbor in protest of British taxes on the colonies. The event becomes known as the Boston Tea Party.

1783

The British sign a peace treaty, bringing an end to the long Revolutionary War.

April 30, 1789

George takes the oath as the first president of the United States from the balcony of Federal Hall on Wall Street in New York.

1747

George moves in
with his favorite half
brother, Lawrence,
and Lawrence's wife
at Mount Vernon.

July 1752

After Lawrence dies,
George inherits Mount
Vernon and takes over
his half brother's place
in the militia.

June 15, 1775

George is put in charge
of the newly formed
Continental army.

July 4, 1776

The Continental Congress
adopts the Declaration of
Independence, taking a
big step toward creating a
separate nation.

1792

George is reelected as
president for his second
and final term.

December 14, 1799

George dies at Mount
Vernon with Martha by
his side.

CHAPTER ONE

In Search of Adventure

At the time of George's birth on February 22, 1732, America was a mostly uncharted and wild land populated by native Indians, with more and more immigrants from Europe arriving in search of new opportunities. George, however, was different from most people right from the start. On his father's side, he came from a long line of tobacco farmers in Virginia. George's great-grandfather John Washington had arrived from England in 1657!

George's father, Augustine (Gus for short), also a tobacco farmer, married George's mother, another native Virginian, Mary Ball, after Gus's first wife died. Mary was anything but a nurturing mother. An orphan by the time she was twelve, perhaps Mary didn't get enough love while she was growing up.

Whatever the reason, she was very mean, and even George's friends were scared of her. As her son grew up, she never changed her difficult and dominating ways. Later, during the French and Indian War, she wrote him a letter right before a big battle saying that she needed butter. George always responded to his mother by being polite, although he kept his distance. In his letters to his mother, he began by addressing her as Honored Madam.

Mary and Gus went on to have five more children after George, named Betty, Samuel, John, Charles, and Mildred. The sibling George was closest to, however, was one of his two half brothers from his father's first marriage. Lawrence, Gus's oldest son, was fourteen years older than George. The classic eighteenth-century cool older brother, Lawrence took George under his wing. Having gone to school in England, he knew Greek and Latin, had

impeccable manners, and wore clothes made for a proper gentleman.

George really looked up to his brother. After their father died when George was only eleven, the bond between the brothers grew even stronger. Because there was not enough money to send George overseas to boarding school in England like his older brothers, he had to get whatever education he could at home.

George loved visiting his big brother and his new wife at their beautiful home. Lawrence

As a kid, George was a whiz when it came to numbers, so he loved math. But he was awful at spelling. He was always ashamed of the mistakes he made in his writing as an adult. Throughout his life, George made an effort to continue educating himself by reading books on all different subjects. Still, he never got over the fact that he didn't attend college.

18

had married Anne Fairfax, the daughter of one of the wealthiest families in Virginia. There was always so much happening and so much to soak in at the sprawling estate called Mount Vernon. So when the young couple asked if he wanted to leave his mother's house and move in with them at the age of fifteen, he jumped at the chance.

Life was wonderful at Mount Vernon for George, a strapping, six-foot-two young man with particularly large hands and feet. In those days, when most men didn't grow taller than five feet five inches high, George must have made quite an impression.

George was born healthy and grew up the same way. He was a terrific athlete; some people said he was the best horse

Life at
Mount Vernon

Situated right on the Potomac River, the
plantation was named Mount Vernon by
Lawrence, in honor of his former commander.
(At it's completion after 1757, the estate was
made up of five farms on about 7,600 acres,
or twelve square miles.) Now that George
was hanging out with the wealthiest and
most important families in Virginia, he had
to act the part. He participated in fox hunts
and elegant balls. He bought fancier clothes
and took dancing lessons. He didn't stop
there, though. He took fencing and music
lessons to become more refined. He also did
his homework. George wrote down a long
list of manners, so he wouldn't forget them
(including not to spit into a fire while meat
was cooking over it).

rider in Virginia—and at that time, riding horses was a big deal. George was anxious to taste real adventure outside the protective walls of Mount Vernon.

When he was only a teenager, George signed up to join the British navy. His plans changed, however, when his mom found out. Although she discovered his scheme at the very last minute, Mary forced him to unpack his bags and stay in Virginia.

Luckily, George found another outlet for his desire to find excitement—and it was right in Virginia! The western part of the state was new to the people who'd originally come over from England. There were no roads through the forests or maps of the rivers, mountains, and fields. The Fairfax family, which owned vast stretches of land, hired George to be a land surveyor. The position required him to measure and record the surface of the **terrain** in order to draw boundaries and maps. At sixteen, he took his first trip as a surveyor. Gone for thirty-one days, he wore the same clothes, bathed in icy rivers, slept on the

From money saved from his surveying gigs, George bought fifteen hundred acres of land when he was only eighteen years old.

ground, ran into a rattlesnake, and later a group of Indians carrying a scalp—and he loved every minute of it!

By combining his biggest passions—adventure and math—George became an expert surveyor. Over the following three years, he completed 190 different surveys of land in Virginia.

George showed a willingness to work as hard as any man—whether surveying land, learning science on his own, or practicing his manners—but in some ways he was still a boy. So it must have been upsetting when Lawrence

came down with tuberculosis, an infection of the lungs that killed many people at that time. The two brothers took a trip to Barbados (the only time George would leave North America) in search of sunshine and sea air, which they hoped would cure Lawrence.

Instead, George got sick! He came down with smallpox, which was another deadly disease, but somehow he beat the odds and survived. Lawrence wasn't as lucky. He passed away in 1752 with his brother right by his side. George wondered how he would continue to follow in his brother's footsteps.

CHAPTER
TWO

Soldiering On

George began his military career right after
Lawrence's death by taking over his brother's
position as an officer in the Virginia militia,
which was the colony's part-time army made
up of ordinary citizens. In 1753, he was called
upon to go with six other people on his first
treacherous 500-mile journey to the Ohio
Valley—a **fertile** area that both the French and
English were claiming as their own.

Getting Settled

The French and the English were the two biggest groups of European settlers in North America. The French, who traded furs and other goods, controlled the Great Lakes area, the Mississippi Valley, and the area west of the Appalachian Mountains. The English, who were for the most part farmers, lived in the thirteen colonies that stretched along the Atlantic coast, including:

Delaware	South Carolina
Pennsylvania	New Hampshire
New Jersey	Virginia
Georgia	New York
Connecticut	North Carolina
Massachusetts	Rhode Island
Maryland	

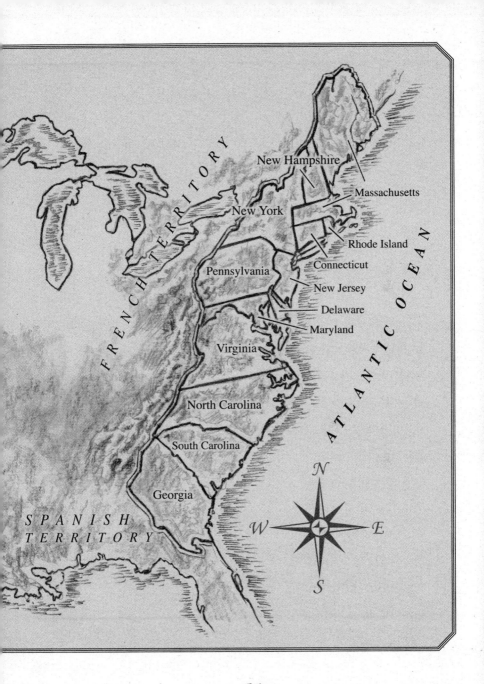

FRENCH TERRITORY

New Hampshire

Massachusetts

New York

Rhode Island

Connecticut

Pennsylvania

New Jersey

Delaware

Maryland

Virginia

North Carolina

ATLANTIC OCEAN

South Carolina

Georgia

SPANISH TERRITORY

N
W   E
S

King George II of England not only wanted to tell the French to get off British land, he also wanted forts built to protect English territories after he found out that the French were **erecting** forts all over the Ohio Valley. George Washington was the man for the mission. During his first trip to the Valley, he chose a spot for the fort that today is

A detailed account of George's first trek to the Ohio Valley, called *The Journal of Major George Washington*, was published in newspapers. His adventures, including being shot at by an Indian who was supposed to be his guide, and having his clothes freeze solid after he was rescued from icy waters, gripped the public and made him famous.

King George II

33

Pittsburgh, Pennsylvania. He delivered King George's threat to get out of the area, which the French commander promptly ignored.

In 1754, with 159 men following his lead, George set out again across hundreds of miles

of harsh terrain into the Ohio Valley. As he and the force of Virginia militiamen marched to drive the French from the region, George knew they'd face hostile Indians, wild animals, cold waters, dark forests, and two mountain ranges.

England's first act of aggression was the attempt to capture the French's biggest fort, Fort Duquesne. George quickly realized that the French were simply too strong for him and his men to overpower. Instead, they built their own stronghold, Fort Necessity, a few miles away.

Fort Necessity did little to protect George and his men on July 3. Seven hundred French soldiers and four hundred Indians attacked George and his three hundred fifty men. In the battle, which marked the beginning of the long French and Indian War, a hundred soldiers on the side of the British died. Washington had no choice but to agree to a humiliating surrender.

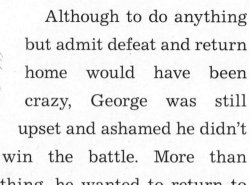

Although to do anything but admit defeat and return home would have been crazy, George was still upset and ashamed he didn't win the battle. More than anything, he wanted to return to the land and prove himself.

He got the chance when Major General Edward Braddock, the British general in charge of fighting the French in the Ohio Valley, made George one of his aides. What a difference it was traveling with the general! When they left Alexandria, Virginia, in the spring of 1755, there were about 2,400 British soldiers, colonial troops, and Indians with them (the line of horses, men, and supplies stretched out for more than six miles!).

George, who was an old pro at the trip by then, tried to warn the general that battles

British soldiers got the nickname "redcoats" from the color of their uniforms. The bright red coats they wore were the opposite of camouflage; the enemy could see these guys coming a mile away!

were fought very differently in America than they were in Europe, where soldiers, facing one another in columns, marched forward, shooting. In the colonies, the enemy shot from behind protective rocks, trees, and anything else they could hide behind.

As George feared, the Indians and French ambushed the British. The three-hour battle

was chaos. Confused by the cries of the Indians and the smoke from hidden French muskets, the English soldiers shot one another, took off and ran, or fell dead. In the end, more than nine hundred men were killed—including the general.

George was unharmed even though his coat was shot four times, his hat was shot once (right off his head), and two horses were killed while he was riding. "The shocking Scenes which presented themselves in this Nights March are not to be described," he said about the battle. "The dead, the dying, the groans, lamentations, and crys . . . of the wounded for help were enough to pierce a heart."

Although he had suffered yet another defeat, George was considered a hero by all accounts for sticking out the devastating battle with courage. At the age of twenty-three, George was given a big position as colonel of the Virginia Regiment and commander in chief of all Virginia forces.

In 1758, the British returned to Fort Duquesne one more time—and of course they needed George to show them the way. No one could have felt too great about facing an enemy that nearly killed them the last time around. By the time they arrived, however, the fort was empty and burning. The French had decided they could no longer protect it. The tides had turned. The British pressed on, and after Britain won a few more battles, the French gave up their claim to the land in 1763. Britain had won the French and Indian War!

CHAPTER THREE

Back to the Farm

When George returned home to Mount Vernon, Lawrence was gone and so was his wife, Anne. When they died, George inherited the huge farm where he had once been so happy. Although he no longer had the presence of his loving brother and his sister-in-law, after the horrors of battle, he was ready to be happy again.

Martha Custis was the key to that happiness. He met the wealthy widow and mother of two

at a cotillion, which was a special ball where couples danced in patterns. The love they developed was warm and friendly. They shared the same values, which centered on a quiet, hardworking life in the country. It was a match.

The couple was married on January 6, 1759, in Martha's house, known as the White House. Both were about twenty-seven years old when they wed. Still, Martha, a small, plump lady, called George "Old Man" or "Papa."

They never had any children, but George treated Martha's two small children as his own. Martha, Jr., who they called Patsy, was two when her mom remarried, and John, known as Jacky, was four. George enjoyed spoiling them by ordering the most beautiful clothes and toys

he could find and shipping them all the way from England. He didn't only show his love for them by buying things. He also worried about their well-being—particularly that of Patsy, who suffered from seizures that were untreatable. (As she got older, the seizures worsened and she died tragically at seventeen.)

Life on the farm wasn't easy for anyone. They had to grow everything they ate and make everything they wore or used (except for fancy things like china, dolls, or carriages that

George the Slave Owner

Part of the reason George and Martha enjoyed leisure and wealth as they did was because they owned three hundred slaves.

Their slaves, like those throughout the southern colonies, had no rights at all. Kidnapped from Africa and brought against their will to a strange land, they were bought and sold. They were treated like property, no better than horses or plows, and sometimes even worse. Slaves were beaten and humiliated to a point where they were afraid to rebel.

Slavery was especially common in the South (there were fewer slaves in the North), because that's where the land was best for farming. The fertile conditions good for growing crops in large quantities gave rise to huge farms called plantations that required a massive amount of labor. When

the plantation owners didn't have to pay the people who worked on their farms, they made a much bigger profit on their crops.

Some of America's Founding Fathers said that slavery went against the country's core value of liberty for all. But others, like George, were slave owners. Racial **prejudice**, the money made from slaves, and strong beliefs in the rights of property owners were all factors that contributed to keeping the immoral institution of slavery alive well past George's time.

In his will, George stated that all his slaves should be freed after he and Martha died. But it wasn't until the Civil War ended with the North winning in 1865 that slavery was finally outlawed from every state.

A Few Other Slave-Owning Founding Fathers

Thomas Jefferson

James Madison

John Hancock

Benjamin Franklin

He owned two slaves who worked on his newspaper but later freed them, and became a vocal opponent of slavery as the president of the Society for Promoting the Abolition of Slavery and the Relief of Negroes.

were shipped from England—and for those, they needed a lot of money from selling their crops).

At first, George followed the example of his father, grandfather, and great-grandfather by growing tobacco. The plant that's used for smoking or chewing is not only a tough crop to grow, but it also robs the land of its nutrients. Never afraid to try new things, George switched over to growing wheat, which he turned into flour. He also started a spinning and weaving business to make material for workers' clothes.

Despite all the effort the huge farm took to keep running and stay prosperous, Martha and George always found time for fun. The couple loved throwing dinner parties and entertaining guests for the weekend. When George wasn't foxhunting, he enjoyed spending time with friends, gambling, listening to gossip, or telling jokes.

CHAPTER FOUR

This Means War

The British won the French and Indian War (thanks in part to George) but it cost them . . . big. Sending all those supplies and troops from England was expensive. England had gone into massive debt for a war over a place most British people would never even see. And they were still paying. England maintained a huge army of redcoats in America just in case the French got any ideas of trying to take back their forts.

In 1760, there was a political change in

England when George III (the grandson of King George II, who pushed for the French and Indian War) became king. The new monarch came up with a plan that the English liked: The colonies should pay back the money for the war themselves, through taxes.

The colonies, on the other hand, didn't like that idea at all.

After the English Parliament passed the Stamp Act in 1765 without any input from the colonies, Americans were forced to pay a tax on every single piece of printed paper they used. That could be anything from newspapers to legal documents to playing cards! The cost of these stamps was as small as a half penny, but it set off a huge reaction. People worried what England would charge them for next if they put up with these stamps.

Americans were okay with paying taxes to their local governments (although the colonies were under British rule, each had its own form of government). But they were not okay sending money to England when they didn't have a say in Parliament. This idea popularized the slogan "No taxation without representation."

The British were surprised by the violent

reaction to the tax. American colonists not only refused to pay it but also stopped buying British goods and eventually resorted to harassing British officials.

A year after passing it, the British Parliament put an end to the Stamp Act— not because they felt bad about what they had done, but because they needed people in America to buy their stuff! In fact, just in

What's So Great About Tea?

Before tea was introduced to the West, Europeans used to wake up and start their day with a mug of beer or ale! After Dutch traders brought tea from Asia around 1610, Europeans were hooked. Drinking tea, which was considered to have healing powers, changed the way they lived. Tea gardens and the ritual of afternoon tea became important parts of society. The opportunity to talk over a nice cup of hot tea was the start of many big ideas and changes in the world. Colonial Americans loved their tea every bit as much as the British. They often drank up to fifteen cups a day!

case the Americans got the wrong idea about their intentions, on the same day Parliament repealed the Stamp Act, it also passed the Declaratory Act, which stated it could make laws enforceable in the colonies "in all cases whatsoever."

As if to prove the point, Parliament soon passed a new law that the colonies had to pay taxes on any paper, glass, lead, paint, and tea imported from England. The same thing happened all over again. The colonialists protested and Parliament took back the taxes on everything—except for the tea.

The tax on tea went too far. Even George, who loved tea just as much as the next colonial American, started drinking coffee instead. Because of the boycott, the amount of tea consumed in the colonies fell from 900,000 pounds in 1769 to 237,000 pounds only three years later.

The export company in London that shipped the 342 chests of Darjeeling tea to Massachusetts still exists today and sells a brew called Boston Harbour.

While George quietly sipped his coffee, others were taking more drastic measures to let their feelings about the tea tax be known. On December 16, 1773, over fifty men, who called themselves the Sons of Liberty, dressed up like Mohawk Indians and sneaked onto three British ships docked in Boston Harbor. Under the darkness of night, they dumped 342 chests of Darjeeling tea into the water. The famous event later became known as the Boston Tea Party.

England took action by shutting down Boston Harbor and the local government.

Redcoats streamed into the city, while town meetings were outlawed. Parliament passed a law that British soldiers could live in anyone's home they chose. With no boats in or out of the city, businesses came to a standstill and many people found themselves with nothing to eat.

The other colonies were angry about what was happening in Boston and resolved to do something about it. They pitched in to help its starving residents. Virginia sent corn and wheat. Connecticut sent sheep for milk, wool, and meat. That helped with the immediate problem. But what about the future?

America needed to do some hard thinking about its relationship to England and what it should be going forward. To debate this issue, the First Continental Congress was created.

Twelve of the thirteen colonies (all except Georgia) sent representatives to Philadelphia in 1774 to discuss America's destiny and show a unified force to England.

From early September through the end of October, the delegates debated about what the colonies should do. Not everyone agreed. Some thought America should seek independence. Others just wanted a better relationship with England. George, who was a delegate from Virginia, wanted to stand up for the people of Boston, but wasn't sure about making a complete break from England.

However, by the Second Continental Congress, in May 1775, George and the rest of the delegates were more resolved that action must be taken against England and readied themselves for war.

The primary reasons were the battles at Lexington and Concord earlier that spring.

Declaration
of Independence

Thomas Jefferson, who would later become
the third president of the United States,
wrote the Declaration of Independence
between June 11 and June 28, 1776. In
it, he basically put forth the idea for a new
kind of government that would protect the
rights that belonged to any citizen. The
Declaration was also an argument for
why the colonies should separate from
England. "We hold these truths to be self—
evident," the document states, "that all men
are created equal, that they are endowed
by their Creator with certain unalienable
Rights, that among these are Life, Liberty
and the pursuit of Happiness." The
Continental Congress debated and revised
the groundbreaking document for four days.
Then, on July 4, the delegates signed the
Declaration of Independence.

When British soldiers were ordered to capture and destroy military supplies, the Massachusetts militia fought back. The combat marked the first open fighting between British troops and colonial soldiers on American soil.

George heard the news about the fighting and wrote to a friend, "[T]he once happy and peaceful plains of America are either to be drenched in blood, or inhabited by slaves. Sad alternative! But can a virtuous man hesitate in his choice?"

CHAPTER FIVE

A Fighting Chance

This was one job George was not sure he wanted.

The Continental Congress asked him to take command of the newly formed Continental army. But George didn't know if he was up to the task. Could he really lead an army against the British? In his military track record, he had more losses than wins. George had little experience compared to the generals on the opposite side, who had spent years training and then out in battles leading the most important army in the world.

Others expressed great faith in him, but that did little to relieve his doubts. Still, in the end, he agreed to become the leader of the new American army.

Army was a loose word for the sixteen thousand soldiers under George's command. Many of them were young (some no older than fifteen!) and poor, with no military training at all. They had joined for the chance to make a little money. They might not have been the cream of the crop, but George was lucky to have anyone join. Throughout the Revolutionary War, there were never enough soldiers and even less food, gunpowder, and clothes to fortify them.

The odds of this scrappy little army beating a world superpower seemed slim to none. The British had more men, more supplies, more money, and more confidence. The Americans, though, did have two crucial elements going for them: They were fighting on home turf, and for a cause in which they believed deeply.

There were many ups and downs for both sides during the Revolutionary War. Americans

earned an important win during the Seige of Boston, on March 4, 1776. George sent three thousand troops during the night to surprise the English, who woke up in the morning surrounded by cannons coming out of the six forts. The British soldiers retreated to their boats and took off. The feeling of victory was gratifying, but unfortunately, George didn't get to savor it for too long.

In late summer, the patriots faced major defeat in the Battle of Brooklyn Heights. Two hundred and fifty-nine soldiers died trying to defend New York, but that was nothing compared to what was coming. In the battles of Fort Washington and Fort Lee that November, almost three thousand Americans were

captured or killed.

The Continental army was down to only six thousand men. On the heels of these devastating losses, many Americans stopped believing in the war. Even George's doubts that he and his scraggly bunch could make any headway returned. But he said, "If I withdraw, all will be lost."

George decided he had to start fighting dirty. That winter he planned a hit-and-run attack on the enemy in New Jersey for Christmas Day. Twenty-four hundred American soldiers, with hardly any clothes on their backs or food in their stomachs, sneaked into enemy territory in the middle of the night to launch a surprise raid. They shot at bewildered soldiers from the safety of houses and anywhere else they could hide. The much-needed win made George realize that if the Continental army was to have any chance in this war, they'd have to plan smaller surprise attacks like the ones he faced with the British in the French and Indian War. It was the only way.

After more battles in Princeton, Saratoga,

and Philadelphia, George led ten thousand men to Valley Forge Pennsylvania, where they'd stay until winter had passed. The point was to

wait it out safely in their camp, but that almost killed them.

The winter and its freezing cold proved terrible beyond belief. There was no heat because all the wood was wet as the men who, wearing barely more than rags, shivered night and day. Many of them didn't have shoes, so soldiers left trails of blood on the snow as they walked. Later, many of their frostbitten feet had to be **amputated**.

Warmth was only one problem. The other was food—specifically that there wasn't any. Soldiers went for days without eating. And many horses were left to starve to death.

In letter after letter, George asked the Continental Congress for supplies to sustain his men. But the makeshift authority didn't have the power to get him the tools he needed. The worst part, though, is that local farmers could have provided the soldiers with food.

Lady Washington

Martha, or Lady Washington, as all the soldiers called her, spent every winter with her husband, camping with his troops. With blood, vermin, and hunger at every turn, it was a far cry from her gracious life at Mount Vernon. But Martha knew her presence, which lifted the spirits of her husband and his soldiers, was important. She did what she could by tending to the sick and offering the men small gifts.

The harvest had been a good one that year, but the farmers chose profit over freedom. They sold their crops to the British in Philadelphia

In order to relax and get a break from his troubles during the war, George liked to play catch.

instead of giving them to the starving American soldiers!

George, who had been a farmer for fifteen years before taking over the Continental army, made up for whatever he lacked in experience with his natural leadership abilities. Though he didn't pal around with his soldiers, instead keeping a measure of distance, his men didn't care. That's because George offered them respect, intelligent guidance, and bravery in battle. He was famous for never showing fear no matter how badly fighting was going for his side or how starving his troops were.

George's strength was surely tested that

winter at Valley Forge, during which over two thousand soldiers died from illness. Disease proved more dangerous than muskets during the Revolutionary War when more American soldiers died of smallpox than from battle. (Luckily, George was immune to the disease because of his bout with it as a young man.)

By May, the weather warmed up—and George received some very good news. The French, who had joined forces with the Americans after they had become the enemies of their enemy, the British, were finally sending soldiers, ships, and money to back their commitment.

With French reinforcements by their side, the Americans experienced victory during that year of fighting. But before they knew it, another cold winter was upon them. If they thought Valley Forge had been bad, the winter of 1779 was a nightmare. With the worst blizzards anyone could remember, the snowdrifts reached as high as six feet. Again, the men suffered without adequate shelter, warmth, clothing, and food. By the summer, fewer than three thousand soldiers were able to fight.

George didn't think things could get any worse, but they sunk even lower when one of his most trusted and important generals turned out to be a traitor. Benedict Arnold, a hero of

Benedict Arnold

the Revolution, was found to be spying for the British! On top of that, the Americans began suffering defeats in the south, in Charleston, South Carolina, and Savannah, Georgia. There was no doubt about it; the patriots were in serious trouble!

CHAPTER
SIX

The End of a War and Start of a Nation

In the end, the Revolutionary War was won with help from George's old foes—the French.

In the decisive battle of Yorktown in 1781, the French and Americans cooked up a crafty plan to corner the British. The powerful French navy sent in their fleet to keep the British, who were in Yorktown, Virginia, from escaping by water. Then troops—led by the nobleman Marquis de Lafayette, who had become a top aide to George and as close to him as a son—

moved in and blocked the English from fleeing by land. Trapped, the British had no choice but to fight.

George and his forces joined the French to start the battle on October 9, firing at the British with everything they had. By October 19, the British had surrendered and were on their way out of Yorktown in what turned out to be the last battle of the Revolution. Tired of fighting a costly war so far from home that they couldn't win easily, the British agreed to sign a peace treaty and let the United States become its own country!

Despite the British surrender, it took two long years to hammer out the details

The eight–year Revolutionary War was the longest in American history until the Vietnam War.

of the treaty. Finally, in 1783, Britain and America signed the treaty in Paris, France, and the United States was officially free and independent.

On November 25 of that year, George triumphantly entered New York City with his soldiers just as the last British troops were leaving. No one was sad to see the English go.

Cheered by crowds along the entire way, George rode down to Annapolis, Maryland, where Congress was meeting, and on December 23, he resigned as commander of the army. His voice choked back the tears, but the men and women around him were not as tough. They cried openly as the hero of the Revolution said good-bye.

On Christmas Eve, Martha got the best present she could have wished for: her husband. George, who was now fifty-one years old, returned to Mount Vernon. Martha and the farm were all he wanted at this point in his life. He had served his country well and earned the right to his peaceful, majestic life. His happiness, though, wasn't complete.

Only a few weeks after the war was won, Jacky died. He had joined his stepfather at the battle of Yorktown, where he got to watch the British surrender. He came down with a fever and died two weeks later, with George by his side.

Jacky had not lived a very successful life. More interested in having fun than working, he was never able to see anything through. He

failed out of college and as a farmer. When he
died, he left four children, two of which, a son
and daughter, went to live in Mount Vernon to
be raised by George and Martha.

George had plenty to keep him busy at
Mount Vernon. Much of the farm needed
updating after his long absence, there was
always a constant stream of visitors, and

now he had two children to care for. Still, his attention kept returning to the young country he'd fought to create and how it still needed people to care for it.

The colonies-turned-states might have won the war, but they still had a lot to do before their new country was assured success. The government was shaky at best, with little authority over all the states. In fact, the United States was less like a country than thirteen separate countries. (Each state even printed its own money!) George recognized that they had to be unified if America was going to be taken seriously by the rest of the world. And he

hadn't fought eight years of tough battles just to see his work go down the drain because of politics.

He didn't want to leave Mount Vernon again (Martha didn't want him to, either), but he knew he had to do his part to help America create a central government with a strong, unifying purpose. So in the spring of 1787, he traveled to Philadelphia to work on the Constitution of the

Branches of Government

The Constitution split government into three separate branches to create a series of checks and balances between them, so that no one part could become too powerful.

EXECUTIVE BRANCH:
The president, vice president, and the Cabinet

LEGISLATIVE BRANCH:
The House of Representatives and the Senate

JUDICIAL BRANCH:
The Supreme Court and all the other courts of the land

United States. Creating a political document that would change the world and how people viewed the role of government was a massive job. The government of a country should work for the people it represents. It took all summer for the delegates to agree to the terms, but by September 17, they voted on a draft of the Constitution that laid out a clear map for running the country.

After the Constitution was signed, George couldn't hop on the next wagon home. There was still work to be done; the country needed a president, and everyone thought George was the man for the job.

On February 4, 1789, the United States of America held its first election for the highest office in the land. Each state chose electors as representatives, who got to vote for the president. George received sixty-nine votes, securing the presidency. John Adams, a Founding Father

and lawyer from Massachusetts, received thirty-four to become vice president.

While most political candidates will do or say anything they can to win an election, George was the exact opposite. In fact, he was

Model President

George didn't want to be president, because he was unsure he could live up to the title. Just as with the Revolutionary War, he had the fate of a country resting on his shoulders. His leadership would help determine if the young nation could develop a strong government. "As the first of every thing, *in our situation* will serve

George Washington

to establish a Precedent," he wrote,
"it is devoutly wished on my part, that
these precedents may be fixed on
true principles." The way he ran the
country became the model for all future
presidents after him.

Presidential Duties:

- serves as commander in chief of
  the army
- creates a cabinet of people, like the
  secretaries of war or the treasury,
  whose job is to give advice
- appoints judges
- decides how the United States
  deals with other countries through
  its foreign policy
- presents a budget for running the
  country to Congress

upset when he learned the news that he was going to be the first president. His aim was to return to Martha and Mount Vernon, not run a country. The people, however, felt differently. They wanted someone brave, loyal, and honest. They wanted George.

As he put his belongings into wagons for the journey to the country's temporary capital in New York City, where he'd be sworn in, he said that he felt like he was "going to the place of his execution."

By the time George finished his four-year term in 1793, he had a full head of white hair. The job of president took every last ounce of energy he had. He suffered two serious illnesses that his doctors worried he wouldn't recover from. Although he was physically and mentally exhausted, everyone from friends to political advisers, including Thomas Jefferson, wanted him to continue on for another four years. The

country was young, and it still needed stability. "North and South will hang together if they have you to hang on," Thomas Jefferson said. Never one to shirk his duty, George reluctantly agreed. In his second election, George won again with John Adams voted vice president again.

At first, George refused to take the $25,000 salary Congress offered to the president, because he had plenty of money. Congress, which didn't want people to think only wealthy men could become president, convinced him to take the money.

The second four years weren't any easier than the first. There were rebellions at home and abroad that threatened America's strength. One aspect of the presidency was a lot of fun for George, and that was planning the nation's permanent capital. He chose a spot named Federal City, conveniently sixteen miles from his beloved Mount Vernon, for the capital (later the name would change to Washington, D.C.). Unfortunately, he was the only president who never got to live in the White House because it still wasn't finished by the time he left office.

That was George's choice, however. There were no laws limiting the number of terms someone could act as president. King George III said that if George left his position willingly, "He'd be the greatest man on earth." Although there were those who still wanted him to remain in the position, George insisted on leaving the presidency after his second term. He wanted to make sure no one confused the president of the United States with a king, and he wanted to go home.

As a young man, George had been desperate for adventure. In the end, he found enough to fill ten lifetimes. He was more than content to leave aside the problems of politics and worry about his wheat, animals, and spinning wheels. He didn't get to enjoy Mount Vernon long enough, however. On a drizzly December day in 1799, George returned to the house soaked after working hours outside in the cold rain. Later that day, he came down with a bad throat infection. Doctors tried to cure him of the disease by draining nearly five pints of blood from his body (a popular treatment back then) and making him vomit with medicine. The doctors' cures probably only made George weaker and worsened his condition. Sometime

during the evening of December 14, after telling Martha that he wasn't "afraid to go," George passed away at the age of sixty-seven.

Martha insisted on a modest funeral, but the nation demanded something much grander to remember the man who led the country into existence. When the Washington Monument was finished on December 6, 1884, it was the tallest man-made structure in the world. Shaped like an Egyptian obelisk, it stands 555 feet 5⅛ inches high with views in excess of 30 miles and is still the world's tallest stone structure. The strong, permanent, and towering monument is a fitting tribute to a leader who, more than two hundred years after his death, remains one of the most respected and beloved leaders the country he founded has ever known.

10 Things

You Should Know
About George Washington

1 George, the eldest of Mary and Gus's children, was always healthy and athletic as a young person—many considered him the best horseman in Virginia.

2 As a teenager, George became an expert surveyor, completing 190 different surveys of land in Virginia over a three-year period.

3 George began his military career right after Lawrence's death by taking over his brother's position as an officer in the Virginia militia, a part-time army made up of citizens.

4 At twenty-three years old, George was made colonel of the Virginia Regiment and commander in chief of all Virginia forces.

5 George married the widow Martha Custis, in her home known as the White House, when they were both around twenty-seven years old.

6 As a delegate from Virginia, George was present at the First Continental Congress in Philadelphia in 1774 to discuss how the colonies should deal with England and all the new taxes it was imposing.

7 At the Second Continental Congress, George was made head of the newly formed Continental army, which he led against the British during the Revolutionary War.

8 George resigned his post with the army less than a month after the last British troops left America in 1783.

9

After being elected the first president of the United States, George went on to serve one more term before stepping down.

10

George died at the home he loved, Mount Vernon, with Martha by his side, when he was sixty-seven years old.

10 MORE Things

That Are Pretty Cool to Know

1 The famous story of George chopping down the cherry tree when he was a kid (and confessing to his angry dad, "I cannot tell a lie . . . It was I who chopped it down.") is actually a lie! An author named Mason Locke Weems made the whole thing up in a book he wrote after George's death to show how honest the president was.

2 Because George and his younger sister, Betty, resembled each other, she would do imitations of her big brother that would make everyone laugh.

3 George had problems with his teeth from a very early age. By the time he was president, he only had one real tooth in his mouth. He wore false teeth made from ivory that hurt a lot. A set on display at Mount Vernon is one of the most popular parts of the entire museum.

4 At the First Continental Congress, George wore his military uniform as a symbolic way to show he supported the move toward independence and the fight it would take.

5 When George returned to Mount Vernon after the Revolutionary War, the king of Spain and the Marquis de Lafayette sent donkeys as gifts.

6 As the most famous man in America, George got a lot of fan mail. Congress passed a law that any letters to or from him could be sent free of charge.

7 When George was president, on Tuesday afternoons from three to four o'clock, any man who was dressed acceptably could show up without an invitation and see or talk to the nation's leader.

8 George's second inaugural address was the shortest in history at only 135 words.

9 Because of his fear of being buried alive, he asked that he not be buried until he'd been dead for two days.

10 To this day no building in Washington, D.C., is taller than the Washington Monument.

Glossary

Amputate: to cut off someone's limb, as an arm, leg, or finger, usually because it is damaged or diseased

Erect: to put up a building or other structure

Fertile: capable of growing many crops or plants

Humility: the belief that you are not better or more important than others, and the ability to recognize your own faults

Liberty: freedom

Prejudice: an immovable, unreasonable, or unfair opinion about someone based on the person's race, religion, or other characteristic

Terrain: an area of land

Places to Visit

Drum up your patriotic spirit by visiting some of the historic places from George Washington's life.

George Washington's Birthplace
nps.gov/gewa

Mount Vernon
mountvernon.org

Fort Necessity
nps.gov/fone

Valley Forge
nps.gov/vafo

Morristown
nps.gov/morr

Washington Monument
nps.gov/wamo

Bibliography

George: George Washington, Our Founding Father, by Frank Keating, Simon & Schuster, 2012.

George Washington: An American Life, by Laurie Calkhoven, Sterling, 2006.

George Washington for Kids: His Life and Times, by Brandon Marie Miller, Chicago Review Press, 2007.

George Washington: Selected Writings, with an introduction by Ron Chernow, Library of America Paperback Classics, 2011.

Inventing George Washington: America's Founder, in Myth & Memory, by Edward G. Lengel, HarperCollins, 2011.

Who Was George Washington?, by Roberta Edwards, Grosset & Dunlap, 2009.

Index

Also Available:

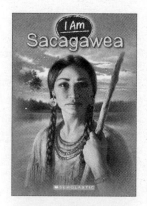

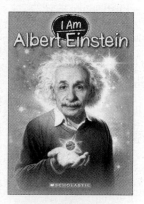